Avalanche!

Christopher Mitten

SCHOLASTIC INC.
New York   Toronto   London   Auckland   Sydney
Mexico City   New Delhi   Hong Kong

Cover photograph
© Mark Jordan/Oi2.com

Copyright © 2001 by Scholastic Inc.
All rights reserved. Published by Scholastic Inc.
Printed in the U.S.A.

ISBN 0-439-31268-X

SCHOLASTIC, READ 180, and associated logos and designs are trademarks and/or registered trademarks of Scholastic Inc.
LEXILE is a trademark of MetaMetrics, Inc.

2 3 4 5 6 7 8 9 10   10 09 08 07 06 05 04 03

Contents

Helicopters are the fastest way to send help
when disaster strikes.

1 Disaster Strikes

The avalanche struck quickly. It hit with deadly force. There was no chance to escape. Tons of fast-moving snow came rushing down the mountain. It snapped trees like toothpicks. It squashed buildings like bugs. And it trapped Anna Conrad in a tomb of ice 20 feet deep. There she stayed for five days.

Anna worked at Alpine Meadows, a ski resort in northern California. It was the spring of 1982. A snowstorm was coming. This was great news. The ski season was nearly over. Snow meant one last chance to hit the slopes.

But officials soon realized that this was no ordinary storm. The snow continued to fall. Ski conditions quickly went from excellent to

AP Photo/Peter Haley, The News Tribune

dangerous. The ski resort decided to shut down. They couldn't take any chances. Not many people could remember a storm this bad. And in weather like this, there was no telling what could happen.

The storm raged for days. Only a handful of employees were left at the lodge. Anna was one. She talked with some friends for a while. That afternoon, she walked into a locker room to change. Suddenly the walls of the lodge exploded inward. Anna was knocked unconscious. When she awoke, she was pinned under a wall of lockers. It was cold and dark. She had no idea what had happened.

A massive avalanche had hit the lodge. It was a huge wall of snow twenty feet high and half a mile wide. Over the next few days, a search party rescued several people. Seven others were found dead. After five days, only one person was still missing: Anna.

Rescuers feared the worst for Anna. The more time that passed, the less likely she would be found alive. But Anna had not given up hope. She was wearing warm clothes. She had

on a jacket, snow pants, and wool socks. She ate snow to prevent thirst. There was not much room to move in her tiny cave. She was bent over. It was as if the avalanche had caught her doing sit-ups. At least she could rub her feet to keep warm. Day after day, she tried to remain positive. She knew help would come— but when?

For days rescuers searched the area. More storms slowed their progress. The lodge had been reduced to rubble. The rubble was covered in snow. Luckily, the rescuers had some help. They had trained dogs to sniff through the rubble. Eventually the dogs led them to the locker room.

Pieces of the locker room were everywhere. Finally, someone spotted a hand. They thought it was another dead body. All of a sudden, the hand moved. Then it disappeared back into the rubble. The rescue workers were stunned. For a moment, no one could speak. Finally, one of them yelled, "Anna, is that you?"

"Yes, it's me," she replied.

Anna was alive!

They worked quickly to free her. Anna was flown to a hospital. She had terrible **frostbite.** She lost half a foot and part of her right leg. But she was lucky to be alive.

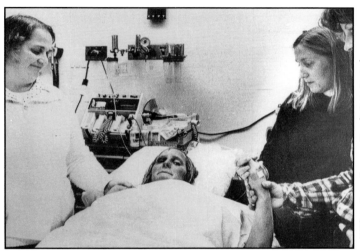

After Anna was rescued, she was rushed to the hospital.

Why was Anna lucky to be alive?

AP Photo/Lance Iverson, Nevada State Journal

2 The White Death

There are over a million avalanches every year. Some are very powerful. They can pack the force of 200 pounds of dynamite! In avalanches like this, there are rarely survivors. That's why they are known as the "White Death."

A snowflake doesn't seem much like a killer. It's tiny and **fragile.** It will melt before you can get a good look at it. But what about tons of snowflakes piled on a mountainside? That's a different story. Nothing can resist the deadly force of those tiny, fragile snowflakes once they are part of an avalanche.

The avalanche that hit Alpine Meadows was enormous. It was made of 65,000 tons of snow. That avalanche was heavier and faster than

Most avalanches happen in the wilderness, far away from places where people live.

thousands of speeding trucks. Together those little flakes have a lot of punch.

So, what causes an avalanche?

Each time snow falls in the mountains, layers of snow pile up. Some layers are thin and crusty. Others are thick and soft. Each layer is different. Some are stronger. Some are weaker. On a steep mountainside, weak layers mean trouble.

When a weak layer is disturbed, the layers above it start to move. Slabs of snow and ice break free. Some are as big as cars. They slide down the mountainside. More layers are disturbed. Soon tons and tons of snow and ice are speeding downhill. This is what we call an avalanche.

Avalanches can also be made of new snow. New snow piles loosely on top of the old snow's icy crust. If the mountainside is steep, the loose snow can start to slide. Sometimes the new snow will stop sliding by itself. Other times it will pick up speed. When this happens, an avalanche can start.

An avalanche can reach speeds of over 200 miles per hour. This is why an avalanche is so

deadly. Imagine a ten-foot-high icy slab moving at 200 mph. If it slams into a building, the building is history!

The speeding snow also creates huge blasts of air. Think of the "whoosh" you feel when a big truck goes by. Air blasts caused by an avalanche are much stronger. The force from the air can knock over buildings before the snow even reaches them.

Avalanche victims who survive the blast find themselves buried in snow. If there is no rescue crew, this means certain death. Snow after an avalanche hardens like cement. There is no air to breathe. Other victims freeze to death. No one can survive for long in an icy tomb of snow.

How can an avalanche start?

3 Know the Enemy

Information is the most important tool people have against avalanches. Understanding snow conditions saves lives. So, **forecasters** study the weather and the snow. They use this information to predict when avalanches are likely to happen.

A forecaster's job is like detective work. It begins with a search for clues in the snow. Bruce Tremper is an avalanche forecaster in Utah. He spends four days a week in the **backcountry** during the winter. This means lots of digging. He digs pits several feet deep to look for weak layers. Remember, weak layers cause avalanches.

Bruce also keeps an eye on danger spots. Places where avalanches occur again and again

Forecasters dig into the snow to look for weak layers.

are called paths. Bruce measures how deep the snow is in avalanche paths. He is especially interested in weak layers there.

Bruce also works from his office. Part of his job is studying weather charts. The charts help him predict when snow is coming. A heavy snowfall can cause an avalanche. He also **monitors** temperature changes. Extreme temperatures cause weak layers. And weak layers can lead to avalanches.

But not all avalanches can be predicted. Forecasters cannot watch every mountain in the world. Plus, the weather is always changing. One day the snow is fine. The next day it's dangerous.

Another problem that forecasters face is people. People don't listen. One big part of a forecaster's job is to educate the public. Forecasters post reports on the Internet. They read warnings over the radio. They send forecasts to TV stations. They do everything possible to spread the word.

But some people just won't listen. Maybe a snowboarder ducks under a warning rope. Maybe a snowmobiler ignores danger signs. Both activities can be deadly. Riding a 2,500-pound snowmobile is a sure way to disturb weak layers of snow. In avalanche paths, this is a big mistake. The snowmobilers won't stand a chance. They'll be buried in minutes. And help can take days to arrive.

So, when a deadly avalanche happens, forecasters try to figure out the cause. The avalanche is like a crime scene. Forecasters

hunt for clues. They dig pits. They look at layers of snow. They examine the position of the snowmobiles. From these facts, they can learn what happened. But by then, it's too late. The avalanche has already claimed its victims.

What clues do forecasters use to predict avalanches?

4 Bombs Away

Avalanche forecasters can find danger spots. They can warn people. But sometimes, this isn't enough. Roads and train tracks need to be kept clear of snow. Skiers need to be kept safe. So, some avalanches need to be stopped before they get started. That's the job of the avalanche controllers.

"Ready on a single," a voice calls out. It's the controller at the front of the helicopter.

"Ready on a single," controller Sam Davis replies. He looks out the hatch. One hand grips a small bomb. When he pulls the wire, the fuse will light.

The helicopter moves to the left. It's just about to pass over a famous avalanche path.

The weather has been storming all week. The snow is piled high. It's ready to give way.

"Pull," the controller calls out.

Sam pulls the wire. He holds his arm out of the hatch.

The controller watches carefully. "Now!" he says.

Sam lets go. The bomb drops into the snow. The fuse continues to burn.

Again, the controller says, "Ready on a single."

"Ready on a single," Sam replies.

"Pull," the controller says.

Another bomb lands in the snow. The fuse burns quickly.

The pilot takes the helicopter a safe distance away. It hovers in mid air. The control team watches silently.

Suddenly the explosions begin. Two bursts of light are followed by two deafening bangs. A cloud of snow rises twenty feet in the air. Trees snap as the snow hurtles down the mountainside. It's an avalanche! The team watches for several more minutes. It's

an awesome sight. Then they move to the next path.

This is how many days begin for avalanche controllers. Up before dawn, they are in the air at first light. They set off a few avalanches. Then they're back in the office before the ski slopes open.

You might wonder what's going on. The controllers are supposed to prevent avalanches. So, why are they going around starting them? Here's the reason: These small avalanches prevent big ones. If there are any weak layers, the bombs cause them to **collapse.** When there's no more snow piled on top of weak layers, there's no more danger.

Avalanche controllers like Sam Davis set off over 100,000 hand bombs each year! Each one packs two to five pounds of deadly dynamite.

Most control teams use helicopters. Other teams ski into dangerous areas to set off small bombs. Often the skiers climb to the top of a peak. From there, they toss bombs into avalanche paths. Sometimes they even lower the bombs down on a rope.

These avalanche controllers are shooting small bombs from this cannon. They're aiming at a snowy mountainside.

What if there's a spot they can't reach on skis? It's no problem. They call in the helicopters. From a helicopter, controllers can see into the steepest avalanche paths. They can drop hand charges with deadly aim.

The other tool controllers use is a cannon. Many avalanche control teams use cannons that once belonged to the U.S. army. In very bad weather a team can spend days shooting small bombs into avalanche paths. During these jobs, they can go through thousands of pounds of explosives.

But controllers are not taking random shots. They work carefully with avalanche forecasters. They know exactly where they are shooting. They know exactly how much explosive to use. Controllers have years of training. And they are also very careful. No one sets off an explosion until the area is completely cleared of people.

Avalanche controllers do most of their work in areas where people live. In the wilderness, nature can take its own course. An avalanche deep in the backcountry hurts no one. It

damages no property. But, places like ski areas must be protected. And keeping the roads clear is important, too. Colorado's highway 550 is avalanche-central. Over 100 avalanche paths cross this road. Avalanche patrols have to monitor this area carefully. It keeps them busy all winter.

Controlling avalanches with explosives has been done around the world for over fifty years. In 1982, there were several avalanche controllers working for the Alpine Meadows resort. When the avalanche finally fell at Alpine Meadows, the avalanche patrol had been hard at work for days.

The forecasters knew avalanches were on their way. And when the time came, they shut down the resort. Then the controllers went to work. They set off explosives in the mountains. They took them up on skis. They shot them from cannons. And they dropped them from helicopters. For almost a week the controllers slammed the mountains with bombs. They went through thousands of pounds of dynamite. But the storm was too

strong. The snow kept coming. And heavy slabs remained hidden. This giant avalanche could not be stopped.

The tragedy at Alpine Meadows teaches a powerful lesson. It reminds us that nature can't always be controlled.

How did the controllers try to stop the avalanche at Alpine Meadows?

5 Life Savers

Sometimes the worst happens. A huge avalanche hits. Some people are killed. Others are hurt. That's when the search and rescue teams fly into action. Their job can be difficult. The disasters they see are often tragic. But sometimes people do survive. Saving a life is a rescuer's greatest reward.

Tom Kimbrough has been through a lot of rescues. One thing he always tells his teams is "Never search for a dead person." What he means is never give up hope. There's always a chance that a victim is alive.

Some people might say Tom is too optimistic. But he has a reason to be hopeful. When he was a young patrolman, he worked

Many rescue teams include trained dogs.

Photo: © Jose Azel/Aurora Quanta Productions

at Alpine Meadows. He was one of the people who pulled Anna Conrad from the rubble. She survived under the snow for five days. But Anna was unusual.

In a rescue, every second counts. Avalanche victims usually die in the first few minutes. The snow hardens like concrete above them. The victims have no air to breathe. For this reason, they must be found quickly.

So, the first thing Tom has to do is get to

the disaster. He has to get there fast. Helicopters can get to a disaster area in minutes. And rescue helicopters are made to fly in stormy weather. If the weather is really bad, the rescuers will go on skis.

Once Tom arrives, he and his team start looking for the victims. With luck, the victims have already been found by other survivors or can signal rescuers themselves. Finding people who are buried in tons of snow is almost impossible. It's like looking for

Photo: © Calvin W. Hall/Alaska Stock Images

a needle in a haystack. Often, trained dogs are brought in to help. Dogs use their sense of smell to find victims.

If victims are found alive, they need to be rushed to the hospital. Crews can do advanced first aid. But most victims have frostbite. They need serious medical care. Quick rescue time can save an arm or a leg. This is why helicopters are **crucial**. They can rush victims to hospitals in minutes.

At Alpine Meadows, a first-rate rescue

Rescue teams spread out in a line to look for victims under the snow.

team saved Anna Conrad. She was buried very deep. But Tom and his teammates never gave up. They searched the area for days. Finally the dogs helped find her. Then they used helicopters to rush her to the hospital. Tom and his team saved her life.

Why are helicopters important during a rescue?

6 Avalanche Alert

It's been twenty years since Anna Conrad was rescued at Alpine Meadows. Avalanche patrols in those days were very good. But today they are even better. Mountain regions are better mapped. Patrols know more about avalanches. Search and rescue is quicker. With every rescue, a rescue team learns a little more.

Technology has also advanced safety. Many skiers and snowmobilers wear a small device that sends out radio signals. The signals make it easy for rescue teams to find victims buried under the snow. Skiers and snowmobilers often carry cell-phones. Now they can report a disaster right away.

Still, avalanche deaths are rising. Why?

People are taking more foolish risks. They ignore warnings. They hike without checking avalanche reports. They drive their snow-mobiles deep into the backcountry without understanding the dangers.

Snowmobilers run the greatest risk. The newest snowmobiles are very powerful. Their machines weigh over two tons. If they cross an avalanche path, they're history.

The solution to the rising death rate is simple. People must use their heads. If people pay attention and follow the rules, they'll have little to worry about. They'll be safe. But if they ignore the warnings? They may be facing down the "White Death."

Why are avalanche deaths rising?

Be a Survivor

How can you survive an avalanche? First of all, it's best to avoid dangerous situations. But if disaster strikes, there are some things you can do.

1. Quickly loosen all equipment. Drop your backpack. Take off your skis. Remove anything bulky.

2. When snow hits, try to "swim" to the top. This is important. Being near the top increases your chances of survival.

3. If you are buried, try to clear an air pocket in the snow around you. You must have air to survive!

4. Try to poke something above the surface. A ski pole, a mitten. Use anything you can to signal your location. This will help rescuers find you.

Glossary

backcountry the wilderness or places with very few people

collapse to fall down suddenly

crucial extremely important

forecasters people who make predictions based on data

fragile delicate, or easily broken

frostbite an injury that results from extreme cold

monitors keeps a watch on something over a period of time